THE UNIVERSAL

SMILE AFFIRMATION AND PRAYER BOOK

By

LELA JACKSON

Published by Hemingway Publishers

Cover design by Hemingway Publishers

Printed in United States

HEMINGWAY
PUBLISHERS

CONTENTS

INTRODUCTION
EMBRACING THE JOURNEY

Welcome to my book! I'm Lela Jackson, dedicated to serving others through human services and public relations for over a decade. Now, as an author, my commitment to human development, social success, and rehabilitation continues. In this book, I'll play the role of your therapist, offering valuable insights. Positive affirmations, thought pattern reprogramming, and prayer have profoundly impacted my life, and I'm convinced they can do the same for you.

I'm thrilled to introduce The Universal Smile Affirmation and Prayer Book. Here, you'll learn how to recalibrate your soul's path and claim your birthright to unity and boundless love. By transforming your thoughts, you can manifest the reality you desire, fostering a more gratifying life.

I firmly believe that after reading this book, you'll unearth a fresh persona within yourself, inviting positive opportunities and experiences that will invigorate your soul, leading to healing and, ultimately, bringing a universal smile to every reader's face. My journey of self-discovery motivated me to create this book centered on thought healing.

This book is designed to assist you in fostering new thought patterns sowing the seeds of healing, forgiveness, love, and the life you aspire to live. Each day, I kick off my routine with affirmations and prayers that align my thoughts and actions with my aspirations. Brimming with affirmations and prayers, this book nurtures mental, physical, and spiritual well-being, guiding you toward your desired reality. Our thoughts play a pivotal role in shaping our lives, and through this book, you'll find the path to unconditional love and unity.

Thank you for joining me on this transformative journey of personal growth and self-improvement.

The Power of Affirmations and Prayers:

Prayer stands as a powerful tool that not only comforts us but also assists in navigating complex emotions, fostering forgiveness, and nurturing healthier relationships. It allows us to draw closer to the divine, embrace His love, and gain a deeper understanding of His purpose in our lives. Through prayer, we express gratitude, seek guidance and forgiveness, and receive inspiration and support. It has become clear to me that prayer holds incredible strength for the mind and spirit during the healing process and in our daily lives.

Positive affirmations serve as another potent instrument that can bolster self-esteem, motivation, resilience, and self-confidence. They contribute to the development of a growth mindset, illuminating ways in which we can support others and fostering inner peace and contentment. Affirmations leverage the power of words to reprogram the subconscious mind, helping to form new habits, break free from negative patterns, and motivate us to achieve success.

Having said that, by integrating affirmations and prayers into our daily routine, we create a powerful combination that leads to profound inner healing, unlocking a life beyond our wildest dreams.

Creating the Foundation for Self-Improvement:

Letting go of the past and fully accepting it is undoubtedly a challenging process. This process demands courage and perseverance. The reason is that our self-awareness is often intertwined with our past experiences, making it hard to move forward. It's crucial to confront these experiences without attaching personal identity to them, allowing them to be released unconditionally. To the same degree, negative thoughts add more to the misery and create a mental prison that can only be escaped by recognizing the subtle influences shaping our approach to life. When we view past events through the lens of our self-concept-fueled emotions, we tend to magnify their impact, making them seem larger than they truly are. In this situation, we must hold on to stillness and be fully present in the moment to set ourselves free. This practice allows us to perceive the past as it was without judgment or resentment. Once we gain clarity about past experiences, the mental prison around them will gradually lose its grip on our physical reality. Undoubtedly, clinging to the past can only cause harm in the present and future, leading to fear and insecurity. By maintaining mindfulness and self-awareness, we can find resolution amidst the turmoil created by our own minds and approach life with a full heart.

I would like to take a moment to ask you, have you ever paused to listen to the narrative your thoughts are weaving? If not, you're not alone - it's quite common to get entangled in our own minds. The Universal Smile affirmation and prayer book aims to guide you in crafting a new, authentic story by incorporating daily affirmations and adopting a more positive mindset. Our perceptions and interactions with the world are significantly influenced by our past experiences and future concerns, which are shaped by our thoughts. However, with the guidance of the affirmations and prayers in this book, you can shape your thoughts and manifest the reality you yearn for. The diverse spectrum of affirmations provided covers a range of themes that can trigger negative thoughts, such as abandonment, trust, self-worth, and more. Instead of dwelling on these sentiments, I encourage you to view them as opportunities for growth and self-empowerment. With the help of this book, you can break free from the cycle of suffering and become the best version of yourself.

I, as your therapist behind the pages, am thrilled to be part of your journey in manifesting your thoughts! By nurturing the seeds of the enclosed thoughts, we can establish new thought patterns that lead to a renewed personality and mental attitude. Through consistent daily practice, we can smoothly replace outdated, disconnected thoughts with fresh, positive ones. Research has shown that positive thinking can slow down the aging process, reduce stress, alleviate inflammation, and contribute to a happier life by diminishing negative thoughts and aiding the body in eliminating toxins. Now, what more reasons do you need to establish thought patterns?

Moving forward, it's essential to remain vigilant of the negative thoughts that can infiltrate our minds and tempt us to abandon our dreams and aspirations. By cultivating a positive mindset and engaging with new ideas, we can continue to evolve and grow, regardless of our age and the intensity of negative thoughts. Let us serve as shining examples of the power of positive thinking and the boundless potential it can unlock within us.

Continuing with the building of the foundation of self-improvement, it's natural to seek positive outcomes from affirmations and prayers. To achieve this, it is essential to approach these practices with pure intentions and embrace change without apprehension.

Let's explore the affirmations and delve deeper into how to apply them. The affirmations featured in this guide activate all seven chakras in your body, manifesting your thoughts into reality. These chakra affirmations induce deep meditation, fostering healing, reducing stress and anxiety, and stimulating energy flow. Balanced chakras unleash powerful energies that enhance your physical and mental well-being, promoting mental clarity and emotional balance. Listed from highest to lowest, here are the seven chakras, along with their corresponding affirmations and functions:

1. Crown Chakra: "I Understand" Affirmations

   Functions: knowledge, fulfillment, consciousness

2. Third Eye Chakra: "I See" Affirmations

   Functions: Intuition, transparency, meditation, trust

3. Throat Chakra: "I Speak" Affirmations

   Functions: communication, expression, creativity

4. Heart Chakra: "I Love" Affirmations

   Functions: Love, acceptance, compassion, sincerity

5. Solar Plexus Chakra: "I Do" Affirmations

   Functions: strength, personality, power

6. Sacral Chakra: "I Feel" Affirmations

   Functions: pleasure, sensuality, sociability

7. Root Chakra: "I Am" Affirmations

   Functions: comfort, safety, energy, stability

To achieve and maintain high levels of productivity and energy, it is crucial to nurture a zest for life. The affirmations included in this book can help you focus on the future and overcome past setbacks. When you yearn for more out of life, you will attract more opportunities and experiences. Investing in yourself through these affirmations will help you witness the transformation of your life in ways you never thought possible. It is imperative to let go of old thought patterns that no longer serve you and replace them with positive ones. It is also vital to understand that the past is behind you and the future lies ahead. Although the process can be challenging, accepting that you cannot control other people, places, or things is critical. By embodying the behavior and mindset of the person you aspire to be in your daily routines, you can make rapid progress toward your goals. It is essential to remember that healing and transforming your reality takes time, patience, and consistency. Try not to get discouraged or frustrated with the process. By following these eight principles, you can liberate yourself from negativity and awaken your soul. With your thoughts and relationships aligned, your dreams can indeed become a reality! I would be delighted to support you in making this happen. Let's turn the page and sow the seeds of new thoughts!

PART I
DISCOVERING INNER HARMONY

Cultivating inner harmony is a transformative journey that demands unwavering consistency, dedication, and mindful self-care. One can integrate practices such as meditation, affirmations, nature immersion, and more to construct a life marked by harmony and balance. It's crucial to recognize that self-care is not a mere luxury but an absolute necessity. Embark on this profound journey of self-discovery and prioritize self-care in your daily routine. Through this commitment, you can unlock the keys to embracing positivity, building self-confidence, cultivating gratitude, achieving balance, and enhancing overall well-being. Deep care for your soul should be at the forefront of your priorities, leading to a fulfilled life on every level.

Inner harmony, at its core, is a state of peace derived from self-acceptance, acceptance of others, and acceptance of the past. Mindful affirmations serve as a potent soul-care practice, capable of dispelling negativity. Daily rehearsals and intentional deep breathing enable you to silence the external noise and turn your focus inward. By immersing yourself in the present moment and observing your thoughts without judgment, you can cultivate a profound sense of serenity and harmony within.

Applying each affirmation that speaks to you in this section through regular practice and mindful meditation can help reduce stress, enhance self-awareness, and create a space for inner peace to flourish.

Daily Balance Prayer:

Today and every day, I wholeheartedly trust that divine order governs my life. I have unwavering faith that all aspects are working together for my good. This day is filled with unique opportunities, and I am eager to seize them. Grateful for divine guidance, I am confident that every action I take will lead me to prosperity. Surrounded by divine love, which empowers and brings peace, I commit to redirecting my mind to positive thoughts whenever it wander. I am a spiritual and mental magnet, attracting blessings and prosperity. Today, I will succeed in all my endeavors, and happiness will be my constant companion. This will be the best day of my life. It is truly wonderful!

1. Embracing Positivity

I am committed to taking charge of my life and crafting my own narrative.

As a vessel for divine love, wisdom, and harmony, I allow the universe to flow through me, bringing balance and blessings. Each moment presents an opportunity to embrace the gifts of the universe and experience the fullness of my being.

Embracing self-love, I embark on a journey to heal my soul and nourish my mind, striving to become the best version of myself.

I relish the feeling of sending a perfect message, liberated from past memories.

Change is inevitable and unstoppable, prompting me to give attention to what truly serves me today.

I attract wisdom, health, and wealth into my life without hindrance.

Recognizing the necessity of solitude until more people understand, I choose happiness as my constant companion.

I acknowledge my enoughness, believing in my limitless capabilities and potential.

Today, fearlessly embracing my true self with confidence and permission, I understand the power of positive, purposeful thinking.

In the beauty of pain transformed into purpose, I feel a stirring within my soul, inspiring me to reach new heights.

As a cherished creation of the divine, I am blessed with infinite love, unwavering strength, and a profound sense of purpose.

Trustworthy of people's feelings, I exist in a state of freedom governed by divine law.

Understanding that blaming myself for others' actions is self-betrayal, I visualize bouncing back from adversity and defeat perfectly.

Believing in the power of positivity, I speak kindly and spread inspiration.

Healing my past becomes the foundation for a beautiful future, free from self-blame.

I embrace my power and determination, acknowledging my limitless strength and resilience.

Filled with love, I radiate positivity and kindness to those around me, recognizing that there is no need to push, control, or force anything.

Grateful and happy, I trust that the universe consistently works in my favor.

Consistency, with no expiration date, has become my guiding principle.

Proud of who I am and the progress I've made, I am confident in my decisions and trust the path I am on.

Perfect just the way I am, I welcome change and new opportunities for growth.

In complete control of my mind, I refuse to let delays or mental blocks hinder my progress.

Determined to forge ahead with confidence and strength, I am fully prepared for this experience.

At peace, I acknowledge that I am exactly where I need to be in this moment.

Worthy of all the love, happiness, and abundance the universe offers, I wholeheartedly welcome it into my life.

2. Building Self-Confidence

I am beautiful, just the way I am.

Today, I boldly step into my authentic self. Confident in who I am and what I stand for, I give myself full permission to shine. By being true to myself, I inspire others to do the same.

Fully dedicated to becoming a better version of myself, I enhance my mindset, personal qualities, and characteristics.

I've built my own happiness, an unassailable fortress that no one can breach.

I acknowledge that betraying myself is tantamount to ignoring my intuition and gut feelings.

I am equipped and confident, ready to conquer any obstacle in my path.

This is my story, and I will craft it beautifully, expressing myself authentically and inspiringly.

I embrace and celebrate all my strengths and weaknesses, understanding they make me unique and capable.

I have the right to be loved and respected,

refusing to settle for anything less.

Believing in myself and trusting my inner voice guide me towards wise choices.

I am grateful for who I am, cherishing every aspect of my being. My uniqueness makes me exceptional.

I radiate positivity and exude confidence.

With confidence and an unbreakable spirit, I have everything I need to achieve greatness and overcome obstacles.

I am exactly who I prefer to be.

No one is coming to rescue me; my safety resides within me.

I am completely healthy, trusting in the law of harmony and order.

I am a positive influence on humanity.

Universally beautiful in every way, I am an
expression of love in this world.

A child of God, I live in harmony with divine laws, drawing strength from this higher power.

Loved according to divine law, nothing can alter this truth.

I always deserve to treat myself with kind-

ness.

Today, I fully accept and appreciate my own value and significance.

I see that the universe is smiling.

3. Cultivating Gratitude

Expressing gratitude to the universe,

I appreciate the smiles life brings.

I am thankful for understanding the power of my thoughts.

I feel fortunate and grateful for all I have.

Cultivating a mindset of gratitude and abundance, I focus on the positive aspects of my life.

I am thankful for a new reality and grateful for life as it is.

Today, I express gratitude for anything and everything that comes my way.

I am still here; thus, I have much to be grateful for.

Saying thank you is a divine expression of appreciation.

Thankful for the simple pleasures and the joy they bring.

I am grateful for valuable lessons and appreciate the opportunity to gain new knowledge.

Grateful for wisdom and health.

Gratitude extends to my progress and the challenges that made me stronger.

Thankful for the abundance

surrounding me.

Expressing gratitude for unique talents and abilities.

Appreciating moments of joy and laughter that illuminate my life.

Grateful for the love and support of family and friends.

Thankful for health, beauty, wonder, and

the freedom to pursue dreams.

PART II
NAVIGATING LIFE'S CHALLENGES

Learning to navigate life's challenges with a positive outlook is essential. By aligning yourself with the flow of life rather than resisting it, you can liberate yourself from the burdens of fear, anxiety, and inner turmoil, discovering joy in the simplicity of everyday life. The affirmations provided in this section serve as powerful and practical tools, empowering you to counteract negative feelings and thoughts about your past or future experiences. Repeat these affirmations boldly while practicing deep breathing, choosing those that resonate with you. Witness as the positive thought seeds you sow drown out fear and anxiety, miraculously healing the wounds of your painful past, shame, or regret.

Universal Prayer

Universal Mind within me, I confidently surrender my worries, anxieties, and small-minded concerns to you. I trust your infinite intelligence to handle them in the best possible way, creating abundant opportunities for me. Innate Intelligence, I release my suffering and self-pity to you, acknowledging my power to transform thoughts and actions. I invite your intervention, guiding me toward a life reflecting my highest potential. With gratitude for your assistance, I boldly declare that everything unfolds wonderfully for me. It is truly wonderful!

1. Overcoming Fear and Anxiety

Today, divine assistance guides me.

In the secret place of the Most High, I find the strength and courage to face life's challenges confidently.

Embracing my flaws, I recognize they make me unique.

I refrain from rushing, understanding I can only do one thing at a time.

Surrounded by divine love and guidance, I am supported.

Acknowledging the transient nature of emotions, I bravely revisit my past.

Recognizing this feeling's impermanence, I am capable of overcoming it.

I am proud of my decisions, and I hold no shame.

I forgive myself.

"I love myself (please mention your full name)."

It's okay to try again.

Supported by family and friends, I trust my-
self.

Positive thoughts banish fear and anxiety.

Proud of my strength and resilience, I am empowered to overcome any challenge.

I understand overcoming my fears empowers me and makes me unstoppable.

Making peace with my past,

fear holds no power.

Confident, competent, and composed,

I remain unstoppable.

In control of thoughts and emotions, I release worries and fears, embracing inner peace.

Worthy of love and acceptance,

I accept myself.

Letting go of expectations, I avoid attachment and disappointment.

Choosing to embrace

my self-worth today.

2. Healing from Within

I allow myself one last visit to the past;

release and healing occur for all involved.

Committed to improving health, I seek divine guidance in all undertakings.

I acknowledge the need for solitude until understanding grows.

Consistency in self-affirmations is the key to inner healing.

Recognizing naivety's potential harm, I request divine guidance.

Inner healing is the first step to freedom.

Growing stronger daily, surrendering allows life to flow effortlessly.

Behaviors and thoughts are my choices.

No one dims my light. I am confident in my abilities and trust in my power to achieve greatness.

Completion doesn't imply negativity; it signifies accomplishment.

Divine love, wisdom, and harmony express through me, bringing balance and equilibrium.

Grateful for shaping experiences I move closer to my desired outcome. My vision is becoming clearer with unwavering determination for positive results.

Avoiding judgment fosters divine connection and purpose.

Trusting my inner journey, I welcome growth.

Pouring positivity into every situation, I drown negativity.

Taking inspired actions clears my path.

Believing everything happens for a reason,

I trust in positive outcomes.

Granting myself permission to heal, I understand truth never denies the seeker.

Seeing things differently, I embrace healing.

Understanding the past is irreversible, I am willing to forgive.

Healing has no deadline.

Aware that my reality is shaped by my thoughts, I smile as a universal medicine.

Open to exploring my inner world, I discover my true self.

Love is expressed at the level of consciousness.

Letting go of stress and tension invites calmness and relaxation.

Strong and resilient,

I release self-blame.

Lovingly letting go of what no longer serves me, I embrace growth.

3. Finding Joy in the Everyday

In the pursuit of joy, I recognize that helping others brings an unparalleled sense of fulfillment.

Commencing each day with a grateful heart and a positive mindset unfolds a beautiful plan for my journey.

I sense that the things I hold dearest are gravitating towards me.

As a beloved child of the divine Creator, I embrace boundless love, strength, and purpose.

Letting go of negative thoughts, I anchor myself in the present moment, where joy can be found.

In this new reality, I’ve discovered a profound love for both myself and the divine concept.

Every day, I vocalize goodwill and harmony, viewing each experience through the lens of love.

Complete and content, I revel in the realization that my happiness is independent of external achievements.

I understand that my behavior and thoughts are my choices.

Happiness is worth a fortune.

Everything is working in my favor, and I am thankful for the blessings bestowed upon my life.

I am purposefully investing in a happier and healthier future for myself.

I love the feeling of being authentically happy.

Guided by the divine in all my undertakings, I discover joy in the simplicity of everyday pleasures.

Today, I choose to surround myself with individuals who bring me joy and happiness.

I carve out time for activities that bring me fulfillment, noting the beauty in nature.

I affirm my worthiness to experience joy and fulfillment.

Today, I will notice nature and find joy.

I am worthy of experiencing joy and happiness daily, acknowledging the abundance of both in my life.

Understanding that self-love is not selfish
but selfless, I remain open to creative
solutions that enhance my well-being.

PART III
STRENGTHENING CONNECTIONS

Honesty and authenticity serve as the foundation for strengthening communication with others. Recognizing the power of words, I embrace affirmations as a means to connect with loved ones, friends, and partners. Words of affirmation nurture unconditional love, forging stronger bonds between individuals. In expressing appreciation for others, a profound sense of value and satisfaction is cultivated, elevating both self-esteem and intimacy.

The thoughts cultivated in my mind wield influence over my actions and reality. Integrating positive affirmations into my life, I embark on a journey of skill development, enhanced relationships, and the spread of love and healing energy. I shape my thoughts and emotions by repeating resonant affirmations daily, cultivating meaningful connections with those around me.

The Oneness Prayer

In unity with my father, the power of God flows through me. My actions are divinely guided, unhindered by any obstacle. Confident in my ability to bring divine completion to my endeavors, I am an extension of God's will. With each step, I am filled with amazement and inspiration, knowing that I am fully supported by the divine. This realization is truly a wonderful feeling!

1. Fostering Healthy Relationships

I prioritize expressing divine love in all my relationships, recognizing its ability to make others feel special.

My commitment is unwavering in creating and nurturing healthy relationships throughout my life.

I understand everyone's opinion is valid

and worthy of consideration.

Embracing humility, I understand that I am not always right and that realization is perfectly acceptable.

A deep sense of trust characterizes my relationship with my partner, creating a foundation of confidence.

Playfulness and flirtation enrich my relationships, infusing them with joy and spontaneity.

I am confident in my ability to make new friends wherever I go.

During challenging times, I do support my friends during tough times.

I am the kind of friend who brings fun and positivity to every gathering.

I love and cherish every moment spent
with loved ones.

I actively encourage others to embrace their higher selves.

I am a friend who appreciates the power of laughter and joy.

In my relationships, I grant my partner and friends the freedom to authentically be themselves.

Dating is a delightful and fulfilling experience that I wholeheartedly embrace.

Confidence resonates within me, assuring the enduring strength of my marriage throughout our lives.

Contentment and happiness define my relationships, as I feel loved, cherished, and fulfilled.

In my romantic relationship, I am both attractive and desirable without the need for control.

I speak my needs and boundaries clearly and respectfully.

I do appreciate the unique qualities of others.

Understanding that love is subjective, I approach relationships with trust and understanding.

I handle people's feelings with trustworthiness and care, releasing internal blockages that hinder love.

I love that my partner is my soul mate, and we love each other purely and unconditionally without judgment.

Sending Love and Healing Energy

Overflowing with love, I am ready to share
it generously with the world.

Embracing the power of love and healing energy, I find fulfillment in both giving and receiving.

Spreading love is a beautiful act that lifts spirits and brightens days.

I am a beacon of positivity, radiating love, vibrant health, and pure joy to everyone I meet. I hope to inspire and uplift others to live their best lives by sharing these gifts.

I radiate love and healing energy in every relationship.

I send love, light, and healing energy to my family, friends, and the universe.

May collective burdens be lifted as we heal, release, resolve, and reset with unwavering love and profound understanding.

My innate ability to spread positivity and inspire others is a cherished gift I strive to share with the world.

May the love and healing energy I send reach those in need, inspiring them to heal and find peace within.

I share love and invite love to fill my life with abundance.

I am open to receiving and providing love and healing energy.

I can fully heal myself, as the power to do so resides within me.

I am a vessel of love, radiating it through every action and word.

I am determined to spread healing, love, good health, and joy to every individual I encounter.

The power within me gives and receives abundantly.

I love that my heart is open and receptive to love and healing, permitting it to circulate freely.

I let love guide my thoughts towards myself and others, witnessing the positive changes it creates in my life.

I understand that people can only give love from their perspective.

I am willing to share my healing energy.

I have the ability to give and express love in
all my relationships, and
I do so willingly.

Consistently sharing love is a timeless practice, helping us learn from each other and grow.

The Universal Smile Meditation

At this moment, I focus on the present and let go of any distracting thoughts that could disturb my inner peace. I am confident and strong in mind, body, and soul, staying true to myself no matter what. Taking a deep breath, I inhale love, wisdom, peace, harmony, and joy and exhale all negativity, worries, and anxieties. With each breath, I send positive energy throughout my being, feeling divine love, beauty, and perfection, saturating my entire being in silence. I know I will receive perfect healing as I am filled with healing energy. Today is full of mystery and miracles, and I am ready to experience them all.

Healing prayers

I have a silent partner, a healing presence who knows how to heal, and its healing presence is bringing about beauty and perfection right now. I believe that my silent partner is saturating my whole being with its love, beauty, and perfection, ensuring perfect healing.

I am healed!!

I believe once and for all that there is but one supreme power, which is all holiness, beauty, and perfection. I know and believe that life's greatest secret is knowing and believing in the one infinitely perfect power. I consciously claim that the healing love of this power that created me is now dissolving all the deposits in my body that do not belong there. I am a temple of the living God, and I glorify God in my body!!!

Conclusion:

The journey of self-discovery and transformation highlighted in this book is an introduction to our next edition, "Empowering the Soul." Embarking on a new journey can be overwhelming, yet it is also an exciting adventure as it lays the foundation for what is to come. We have meticulously crafted the "Universal Smile from Self to Soul" affirmation and prayer book. I strongly believe that this book, will guide your journey towards the next edition, "Empowering the Soul". This book will sow the seeds of positive thoughts, which will help you cultivate a new reality that is filled with abundance.

This book is just the beginning of your journey with the Universal Smile affirmation and prayer book. Inside, you'll find affirmations designed to help you connect with your true self and replace old fears and negative thoughts with powerful affirmations of freedom, right action, confidence, and unconditional love. We understand that absorbing and applying these ideas may take time, so we're taking things slow. Remember to affirm these positive messages to yourself and notice how your thoughts gradually shift.

We're thrilled to continue this journey with you and assist you in creating a new reality for yourself.

Printed by Libri Plureos GmbH in Hamburg,
Germany

9 798869 118783